*THE HARDY*
*The Hardy presents*

# WHERE NOTHING ARRIVES
by **Abram Rooney**

*WHERE NOTHING ARRIVES was first performed at the Tristan Bates Theatre, Covent Garden on Tuesday 29th July 2014.*

**Published by Playdead Press 2014**

© Abram Rooney 2014

Abram Rooney has asserted his rights under the Copyright, Design and Patents Act, 1988, to be identified as the author of this work.

A CIP catalogue record for this book is available from the British Library.

ISBN 978-1-910067-18-5

Caution
All rights whatsoever in this play are strictly reserved and application for performance should be sought through the author before rehearsals begin. No performance may be given unless a license has been obtained.

This book is sold subject to the condition that it shall not by way of trade or otherwise, be lent, resold, hired out, or otherwise circulated without the publisher's prior consent in any form of binding or cover other than that in which it is published and without a similar condition including this condition being imposed on the subsequent purchaser.

Printed by BPUK

**Playdead Press**
**www.playdeadpress.com**

**WHERE NOTHING ARRIVES**
by **Abram Rooney**

Cast
*Chimp*          **Nicholas Armfield**
*Knuckle*       **Peter Watts**


*Director*        **Andy Bewley**

## THE COMPANY

### NICHOLAS ARMFIELD *(Chimp)*
Nicholas graduated from the *University of York* with a BA in writing, directing and performance.

Theatre Credits at university include *Jesus* in *Jesus Christ Superstar*, *Richard III* in *Richard III*, *Dakin* in *The History Boys*, *Speed-the-Plow*, *The Illusion*, *Motortown*, *Woman Beware Woman*, *Betrayal* and *Posh*.

### ANDY BEWLEY *(Director)*
Andy trained at *The Oxford School of Drama,* he graduated for the *University of York in 2014.*

Credits as director include an award winning production of *Jesus Christ Superstar, Immaculate* and *My Mate Tom*

Credits as assistant include *A Number* (York Theatre Royal)

### ABRAM ROONEY *(Writer)*
Abram trained as an actor at *The Oxford School of Drama*, graduating in July 2013.

Theatre Credits include *Christopher* in *Curious Incident of the Dog in the Night-Time* (National Theatre) and *Life on a Plum* (Nabokov) Television credits include *Doctors.* Film credits include *Pride.*

He trained as a writer as part of *Soho Theatre Young Writers Lab* 2013. Short plays include *Could We* and *Sidelines* (The Hardy). Plays include *Where Nothing Arrives* (Camden Fringe) and *The Snow Goose Diaries* with Brian Theodore Ralph (Pulse Fringe). He is founder, actor, writer and director of *The Hardy*.

**PETER WATTS** *(Knuckle)*
Peter trained with the *National Youth Theatre of Great Britain*.

Theatre Credits include *Hamlet in Hamlet* (The York Shakespeare Project), *The Rain King* (Tour), *Oddball* (The Lost Theatre), *A Christmas Carol* (Nightshade Theatre), *As You like It* (York Theatre Royal)

**THE HARDY**
*A theatre movement supporting, producing and experimenting in various forms of contemporary theatre.*

**Founder**             Abram Rooney
**Associate Director**  Jamie Jackson
**Producer**            Holly Hardy
**Dramaturg**           Ben Weatherill

thehardy.co.uk
maketheatre@thehardy.co.uk

## Writers Note

*'I'm a big believer in quiet minds.'*

When I read the blurb of this first ever production of *Where Nothing Arrives* I was struck by this line of dialogue which Andy, the director, had pulled from the text. I was somewhat shocked how it resonated with me. He'd fired my own words back at me and reminded me where this play had come from; and in effect captured the essence of the piece.

I don't know how good my play is but this line reassures me that I've put heart and soul in to it.

It is quiet and I hope visceral text, which explores themes of boredom, masculinity and modern living.

I'm incredibly proud that this production brings together a group of emerging artists at the very start of their careers. I hope that this combined vitality will make for an exciting outcome, raw and honest.

*Abram Rooney 2014*

***Where Nothing Arrives***

*for my Father*
*for my Brothers*


*The spirit of this play is in part inspired by the song Nothing Arrived by The Villagers.*


*"Not with a bang but a whimper"*
*T.S. Elliot*

**Characters**

**CHIMP**      Early Twenties
**KNUCKLE**    Early Thirties

*The building site of an unfinished house in Kensal Rise, London.*

*Present Day*

*A half built new build in Kensal Rise. It is the dead of night in late September. Silence hangs.*

**CHIMP.** Everyone's got to have enough pain before they stop/ don't they

**KNUCKLE.** Do you know what I'd like

*CHIMP shakes his head.*

**KNUCKLE.** A beautiful woman possibly naked but not even…to stand in front of me and- I won't go looking for it I won't…

*CHIMP nods.*

**KNUCKLE.** Even though that's all I'd like

**CHIMP.** -

**KNUCKLE.** -

**CHIMP.** Love to know how many times Jamie's shagged that bird

**KNUCKLE.** never

**CHIMP.** course he has

**KNUCKLE.** definitely not never no

**CHIMP.** obviously he has

**KNUCKLE.** reckon he has do you?

**CHIMP.** Blatantly

**KNUCKLE.** No Chimp.

**CHIMP.** Alright

**KNUCKLE.** No no

**CHIMP.** Alright

*Silence.*

**KNUCKLE.** What did you mean before then- what was it you were…

**CHIMP.** oh

**KNUCKLE.** About pain and that

**CHIMP.** Just how you know we all need to have had pain or whatever before we stop

*KNUCKLE nods.*

*Silence.*

**CHIMP.** Time?

**KNUCKLE.** Same

**CHIMP.** Well no it's not what's the time?

*KNUCKLE begrudgingly checks his watch.*

**KNUCKLE.** Four

**CHIMP.** What four exactly?

**KNUCKLE.** Excuse me?

**CHIMP.** Is it/ four on the dot?

**KNUCKLE.** I just said didn't I?

**CHIMP.** Yeah but is it like/ you know

**KNUCKLE.** I don't really think…

**CHIMP.** Is it four/ on the dot

**KNUCKLE.** …it matters whether or not-

**CHIMP.** Cos if it is well… if it is-

**KNUCKLE.** Look at that

**CHIMP.** Yeah great

**KNUCKLE.** That there is the hand of genius

**CHIMP.** It's a hand alright

*Silence.*

**KNUCKLE.** That is the hand of a genius

**CHIMP.** Right

**KNUCKLE.** –

**CHIMP.** –

**KNUCKLE.** Just know it

**CHIMP.** Okay I know it

**KNUCKLE.** yeah don't you fucking know it

**CHIMP.** Yeah I fucking know it

**KNUCKLE.** Good.

**CHIMP.** Yeah good

**KNUCKLE.** Good

**CHIMP.** Good

**KNUCKLE.** alright

**CHIMP.** Alright

**KNUCKLE.** yeah yeah that's enough

**CHIMP.** yeah yeah that's enough

**KNUCKLE.** Really?

**CHIMP.** Really?

**KNUCKLE.** Okay

**CHIMP.** Okay

*Silence.*

**KNUCKLE.** Oh dear I'm bored you know I am I am f'ing bored

*Silence.*

**CHIMP.** Give us a clue

**KNUCKLE.** no clues

**CHIMP.** but fucking why not

**KNUCKLE.** The fuck was that

**CHIMP.** just tell me

**KNUCKLE.** Sound like a bird being humped by a dog just then you fucking nancy boy

**CHIMP.** A bird being humped by a dog

**KNUCKLE.** So what

**CHIMP.** Why a dog

**KNUCKLE.** why the fuck not smart arse

**CHIMP.** It'd just kill it

**KNUCKLE.** Kill what

**CHIMP.** the bird

**KNUCKLE.** What bird

**CHIMP.** the bird

**KNUCKLE.** saying the bird!

**CHIMP.** the bird you just

**KNUCKLE.** Give it a rest will you

**CHIMP.** But you just

**KNUCKLE.** give it a rest

*Silence.*

*CHIMP takes out a packet of smart looking Cashew nuts.*

**CHIMP.** Gourmet

**KNUCKLE.** what is

**CHIMP.** that's my point

**KNUCKLE.** what's your point what you going on about gourmet

**CHIMP.** what does it mean cos-

**KNUCKLE.** it means special don't it

**CHIMP.** Does it cos-

**KNUCKLE.** obviously it does

**CHIMP.** Nah

**KNUCKLE.** what do you mean nah

**CHIMP.** it doesn't

**KNUCKLE.** course it does

**CHIMP.** Doubt it

**KNUCKLE.** You'd know would ya

**CHIMP.** Maybe

**KNUCKLE.** Maybe?

**CHIMP.** Yeah

**KNUCKLE.** How

**CHIMP.** what do you mean how

**KNUCKLE.** How would you know

**CHIMP.** Cos I would

**KNUCKLE.** for fuck sake

**CHIMP.** What now

**KNUCKLE.** you and your you are just- aren't you and you never well you never-

*Silence.*

**CHIMP.** Sorry

*Silence.*

*KNUCKLE itches loudly.*

**CHIMP.** what are you doing

**KNUCKLE.** Beard

**CHIMP.** you look like a dog

**KNUCKLE.** so do you

**CHIMP.** no but you look like an animal

**KNUCKLE.** I am an animal

**CHIMP.** you know what I mean

**KNUCKLE.** I know that I'm animal and I know I've got an itchy beard but that's all I know thank you very much

**CHIMP.** Yeah

**KNUCKLE.** Shut up

**CHIMP.** walked in to that one

**KNUCKLE.** maybe I did

*Beat*

**CHIMP.** I wish they'd give us beer

**KNUCKLE.** what do you want beer for

**CHIMP.** because I want some fucking beer alright

**KNUCKLE.** don't need any beer

**CHIMP.** I do

**KNUCKLE.** no what you fucking need is some patience

**CHIMP.** how'd you work that out

**KNUCKLE.** patience and some fucking self-restraint

**CHIMP.** I've got self-restraint

**KNUCKLE.** oh yeah

**CHIMP.** Have

**KNUCKLE.** Okay

**CHIMP.** I have

**KNUCKLE.** believe you

**CHIMP.** No but-

**KNUCKLE.** I'm not saying-

**CHIMP.** you are –

**KNUCKLE.** No I'm fucking not

*Pause.*

**KNUCKLE.** I'm not

**CHIMP.** Fine

**KNUCKLE.** Baby

**CHIMP.** Not being a baby

**KNUCKLE.** Well you are

**CHIMP.** fuck you

**KNUCKLE.** oh dear that was below the belt wasn't it there – poor shot – dirty shot – below the bar – under par – not nice that there Harry lad not nice

**CHIMP.** Don't call me that

**KNUCKLE.** it's your name

**CHIMP.** no it's not

**KNUCKLE.** but it is

**CHIMP.** Not

**KNUCKLE.** Okay

**CHIMP.** it's not my name so don't call me it

**KNUCKLE.** Okay

**CHIMP.** I mean it

**KNUCKLE.** I said Okay

*Pause.*

**KNUCKLE.** But it is your name and you are going to have to face that one day

**CHIMP.** IT IS NOT MY FUCKING NAME! Okay?

**KNUCKLE.** Alright then

**CHIMP.** –

**KNUCKLE.** But it is

*Silence.*

**KNUCKLE.** what I don't understand is why you don't just use the fucking name

**CHIMP.** Because… it's/ not my name

**KNUCKLE.** I mean Harry is a Princes name

**CHIMP.** but not mine so

**KNUCKLE.** Alright… alright – pass us the chocolate

*Silence.*

**CHIMP.** you had quite a lot of that

**KNUCKLE.** had half… you have half

**CHIMP.** just like you- that though

**KNUCKLE.** yeah well I didn't have any of the cashews

*Silence.*

*CHIMP drinks some sparkling water and chokes.*

*KNUCKLE laughs.*

**CHIMP.** I really thought I was gonna die

**KNUCKLE.** don't be such a pussy

**CHIMP.** no I'm serious

*Silence.*

**CHIMP.** do you want to die?

**KNUCKLE.** no choice

**CHIMP.** you know what I mean

*Beat*

**KNUCKLE.** Yes

**CHIMP.** Do ya...? I don't

**KNUCKLE.** Course you do

**CHIMP.** No! I don't

**KNUCKLE.** Course you fucking do

**CHIMP.** How'd you know?

**KNUCKLE.** You as an old fucking man crawling round the place with a fucking hunch back you wouldn't last two fucking seconds you can barely do anything now – no no – you'll want to die

**CHIMP.** Oh!

**KNUCKLE.** believe me when the time comes

**CHIMP.** Sorry but

**KNUCKLE.** You'll be fucking begging him to take you

**CHIMP.** What you believe all that?

**KNUCKLE.** No…but I'm saying- *you* will

**CHIMP.** Won't

**KNUCKLE.** Will when you ain't got no one else

**CHIMP.** What's that mean – I'll have Sal

**KNUCKLE.** Not by then

**CHIMP.** -

**KNUCKLE.** She'll leave – once she's seen your balls drop to the floor like they will

**CHIMP.** My balls won't- my balls-

**KNUCKLE.** Are big- I've seen them – yeah gravity gonna get them Chimp

*Silence.*

**CHIMP.** Like to be cremated

**KNUCKLE.** Wouldn't

**CHIMP.** Yes I would

**KNUCKLE.** Just said you didn't want to die

**CHIMP.** No choice

**KNUCKLE.** Jesus Christ

**CHIMP.** If I had to go any way I'd be cremated

**KNUCKLE.** What you mean go anyway

**CHIMP.** Cremated

**KNUCKLE.** That's what they do after you die you fucking twollop

**CHIMP.** Yeah… I know

**KNUCKLE.** So what do you mean that's the way you'd like to go- you're already gone by that stage

**CHIMP.** What is

**KNUCKLE.** You – your soul or whatever

**CHIMP.** Yeah exactly I'm talking about my body though

**KNUCKLE.** Shut up

**CHIMP.** About my body

**KNUCKLE.** Yeah I get it Chimp-face - I get it

*Silence.*

**KNUCKLE.** This fucking beard

**CHIMP.** Not really a beard

**KNUCKLE.** More beard than what you've got

**CHIMP.** Never said-

**KNUCKLE.** ain't

**CHIMP.** Well I never...

**KNUCKLE.** No come on

**CHIMP.** Whatever!

**KNUCKLE.** No go on say it

**CHIMP.** –

**KNUCKLE.** Say I can't grow hair on my face

**CHIMP.** Dick

**KNUCKLE.** Dick?

**CHIMP.** –

**KNUCKLE.** Where would you be…without me… gotta ask yourself

**CHIMP.** I do

**KNUCKLE.** What's that

**CHIMP.** Nothing

**KNUCKLE.** Smart Alec you ain't you- sometimes- but I put up with it – don't I

**CHIMP.** What do you want a fucking/ medal

**KNUCKLE.** Yeah I would yeah

**CHIMP.** Well…you better er right yeah look up your arse then eh!

*Pause.*

**KNUCKLE.** That was very poor effort that there Harry very poor – cos that did not…at all in the slightest

**CHIMP.** Did

**KNUCKLE.** No. You see. It didn't

**CHIMP.** –

**KNUCKLE.** No no I er respect you for

**CHIMP.** –

**KNUCKLE.** Having a go and that

*Pause.*

**KNUCKLE.** Finished that chocolate have you

**CHIMP.** Said I could

**KNUCKLE.** Alright it was just a question – I was merely being… for Goodness sake… no need to bite my head off… just curiosity… all that was was a… a light little wondering… upon the chocolate related stock up… keeping of… so like

*Silence.*

**CHIMP.** Give us a clue

**KNUCKLE.** Told you no clues

*Silence.*

*CHIMP has found a penny on the floor.*

*He picks it up.*

*Holds it up.*

*Looks at it.*

*Spits on it.*

*Shines it up.*

**CHIMP.** Where would you go if you had you know- all the money

**KNUCKLE.** Wouldn't

**CHIMP.** No. You've won all the money

**KNUCKLE.** Why waste it

**CHIMP.** No. But you wouldn't be able to – waste it

**KNUCKLE.** I'd invest it

**CHIMP.** No. But you've got an endless stream

**KNUCKLE.** Keep on investing it

**CHIMP.** Wouldn't spend any of it?

**KNUCKLE.** Not a penny

**CHIMP.** I would

**KNUCKLE.** We know…/no restraint

**CHIMP.** I'd buy one of everything… buy a car first

**KNUCKLE.** Oh yeah?

**CHIMP.** Yeah… a nice sports type one

**KNUCKLE.** What like a… Ferrari – do/ you mean?

**CHIMP.** No I mean like a formula one style kind of you know

**KNUCKLE.** Really would you? Wouldn't know what to do with a car like that you

**CHIMP.** Go on holiday too

**KNUCKLE.** Be like putting a sardine in a matchbox

**CHIMP.** Somewhere hot

**KNUCKLE.** Oh would you!

**CHIMP.** Yeah? Somewhere sunny

**KNUCKLE.** –

**CHIMP.** Like the Caribbean

**KNUCKLE.** Oh yeah?

**CHIMP.** Yeah

**KNUCKLE.** Right yeah… yeah

**CHIMP.** You'd like that would you?

**KNUCKLE.** What? Oh… you'd… you're inviting me?

**CHIMP.** Only if you want to

**KNUCKLE.** The Caribbean

**CHIMP.** Yes to the Caribbean

**KNUCKLE.** Yeah… where 'bouts

**CHIMP.** I… dunno

**KNUCKLE.** –

**CHIMP.** Just a beach – you know

**KNUCKLE.** It's got... coconuts

**CHIMP.** Er- sure yeah

**KNUCKLE.** Okay yeah... love to

**CHIMP.** Oh so you wanna join me

**KNUCKLE.** Yeah okay I'll join ya...I'll joining ya if you promise not to talk so much

**CHIMP.** Alright deal

**KNUCKLE.** I'm there

**CHIMP.** It's settled then

*Pause.*

*KNUCKLE chuckles to himself.*

*CHIMP sways.*

**KNUCKLE.** What else would you buy?

*CHIMP sways.*

**CHIMP.** All sorts

**KNUCKLE.** Like what

**CHIMP.** Er- stuff

**KNUCKLE.** Like

**CHIMP.** Tablecloths

**KNUCKLE.** What else

**CHIMP.** Beds

**KNUCKLE.** –

**CHIMP.** Lamps… fancy ones… and food… exotic fruit and veg buy boxes of hemp… and a crate of whey powder

**KNUCKLE.** What'd you want whey powder for?

**CHIMP.** Hench

**KNUCKLE.** Good luck

**CHIMP.** Get a dog too

**KNUCKLE.** Already got a dog

**CHIMP.** Real one

**KNUCKLE.** You have got –

**CHIMP.** No I know but

**KNUCKLE.** He is real fucking dog the poor sod what do you mean-

**CHIMP.** No I mean like a fancy one

**KNUCKLE.** Fancy dog

**CHIMP.** Like a celebrity style one

**KNUCKLE.** It's not a fucking haircut chimp lad it's a fucking dog you're talking about I mean

*Pause.*

*KNUCKLE thinks on this deeply.*

*Chimp is shaking.*

**KNUCKLE.** What you got in mind?

**CHIMP.** Dunno

**KNUCKLE.** Dunno?

**CHIMP.** Husky probably

**KNUCKLE.** Oh yeah

**CHIMP.** –

**KNUCKLE.** I had a husky

**CHIMP.** –

**KNUCKLE.** Beautiful

**CHIMP.** That's what I'm saying

**KNUCKLE.** Bizlay

**CHIMP.** –

**KNUCKLE.** She was called

**CHIMP.** Bizlay?

**KNUCKLE.** Yes sir

**CHIMP.** What does it mean?

**KNUCKLE.** Not a thing

**CHIMP.** Where's it from – the name

**KNUCKLE.** It's not from anywhere I made it up

**CHIMP.** –

**KNUCKLE.** Was gorgeous

**CHIMP.** Where'd you get her?

**KNUCKLE.** Billy

**CHIMP.** Billy use to breed huskies did he… never knew that

**KNUCKLE.** Course you didn't you've no curiosity about you

**CHIMP.** Have

**KNUCKLE.** Haven't

**CHIMP.** I have I am curious

**KNUCKLE.** You're not you don't look past your own nose

**CHIMP.** I do

**KNUCKLE.** No…

**CHIMP.** I do

**KNUCKLE.** No you don't. And you get bored because of it

*Pause.*

*CHIMP crouches against the wall.*

**CHIMP.** Well that's true

**KNUCKLE.** –

**CHIMP.** Maybe you're right

**KNUCKLE.** I know it

**CHIMP.** –

**KNUCKLE.** You get bored don't you all the time- every girl before Sal

**CHIMP.** No yeah

**KNUCKLE.** It's true isn't it it's true

**CHIMP.** No you're right it's true

**KNUCKLE.** I know it

**CHIMP.** You're right I do – I mean not with Sal

**KNUCKLE.** A bit with Sal

**CHIMP.** Yeah maybe a bit with Sal yeah

**KNUCKLE.** You have

**CHIMP.** Not yet

**KNUCKLE.** Bit

**CHIMP.** Maybe a bit yeah

**KNUCKLE.** It's the year mark with you

**CHIMP.** What is

**KNUCKLE.** The boredom

**CHIMP.** –

**KNUCKLE.** You're fine cos everything is there how it's…but then you stop getting curious with them or about them you know – at the year mark – you start getting all – don't you – all- and then that's it- downward spiral from then on

**CHIMP.** It's true – how do you –

**KNUCKLE.** I've been round the block Chimp lad I've seen things I have seen all sorts of things and I know boredom more than any other thing

**CHIMP.** Yeah

**KNUCKLE.** Oh yes. I know it like the back of my hand boredom in relationships… I had to learn to stay curious not just see what's in front of my nose… "Oh done that on to the next thing" you got to keep digging further

**CHIMP.** –

*Silence.*

**CHIMP.** Why do you think that is?

**KNUCKLE.** No idea

**CHIMP.** You think it's to do with – or whatever

**KNUCKLE.** With

**CHIMP.** You know

*KNUCKLE shakes his head.*

**CHIMP.** Maybe it's to do with my dad you know

**KNUCKLE.** What on earth are you going on about?

**CHIMP.** You know like they say it's to do with you're childhood or whatever

**KNUCKLE.** What? You getting bored with your missus is to do with you being unable to communicate with your father?

**CHIMP.** No about me not staying curious maybe

**KNUCKLE.** Your father was emotionally constipated

**CHIMP.** –

**KNUCKLE.** Everyone knew that

**CHIMP.** –

**KNUCKLE.** Said it

**CHIMP.** –

**KNUCKLE.** That wasn't your fault that

**CHIMP.** –

**KNUCKLE.** Wouldn't stop you being curious no no the boredom…?

**CHIMP.** ?

**KNUCKLE.** You're to blame with that one

**CHIMP.** –

**KNUCKLE.** And you'll never learn

**CHIMP.** I-

**KNUCKLE.** Think about it

**CHIMP.** –

**KNUCKLE.** You're to blame

**CHIMP.** Maybe you're-

**KNUCKLE.** I know I am

**CHIMP.** Yeah

**KNUCKLE.** I am I know

**CHIMP.** No yeah

**KNUCKLE.** –

**CHIMP.** ?

**KNUCKLE.** But. You can fix it

**CHIMP.** ?

**KNUCKLE.** First. First you have to recognise it

**CHIMP.** –

**KNUCKLE.** Which to be fair to ya well to be fair to ya you've gone and done that there so

**CHIMP.** I have

**KNUCKLE.** No I know that's what I'm saying you have to be fair and that's progress proper progress and that's what I've always liked about you Chimp you've got that in you the ability to see something wrong in yourself it's a very human quality of yours… I like that always wish I had more of that – from you

*Silence.*

**KNUCKLE.** Now let me give you an example…a less focused man would be lonely

**CHIMP.** –

**KNUCKLE.** A less focused man than *myself*. Would have succumbed to lust or greed by now

**CHIMP.** –

**KNUCKLE.** Not me

**CHIMP.** –

**KNUCKLE.** Oh no

**CHIMP.** –

**KNUCKLE.** But you- you've succumbed to lust before now and greed and you know that as well as I do

**CHIMP.** 'snot fair

**KNUCKLE.** Now come on you've admitted that much to me before

**CHIMP.** That was-

**KNUCKLE.** I'm just saying – for the sake of argument – I think it's best to have it all out/ in the

**CHIMP.** Yeah alright then fair enough

*Pause.*

**KNUCKLE.** Now I myself as you know lost my one and only love two autumns ago and you know that well it's safe to say that a less hard working honest man would have submitted would have lost himself down the wrong road Chimp not me

**CHIMP.** –

**KNUCKLE.** I've not been down Leyways no I've not pulled up on any curbs not gonna sniffing around the backstreets no no not I

**CHIMP.** I haven't either

**KNUCKLE.** No one's saying you have Chimp

**CHIMP.** But

**KNUCKLE.** No ones saying you have

**CHIMP.** –

**KNUCKLE.** What we are saying what we are investigating Chimp cos that's what we're doing here that's what we are always pursuing isn't eh Chimp? What we are exploring here is what the…possibilities of yourself in this position is and what the likely… consequences may be that might then… arise from these actions

**CHIMP.** Of course

**KNUCKLE.** That's what this is really about isn't it Chimp

**CHIMP.** Yeah no

**KNUCKLE.** The possibilities

**CHIMP.** Of course the possibilities absolutely

**KNUCKLE.** There we are see

**CHIMP.** –

**KNUCKLE.** You're coming see… through it now… acceptance… brilliant… well done

**CHIMP.** Thank you

**KNUCKLE.** Denial is a horrible thing now we both know what denial done to me and we know what the consequences of said denial can be. We've seen it with our own eyes. Haven't we… Haven't we?

**CHIMP.** We have

**KNUCKLE.** Yes. You're right. We have.

*Silence.*

**KNUCKLE.** So that's all I'm saying to you about that

**CHIMP.** Right

**KNUCKLE.** Good

**CHIMP.** Thanks

**KNUCKLE.** –

*Silence.*

**CHIMP.** Funny

**KNUCKLE.** ?

**CHIMP.** Life

**KNUCKLE.** –

*Silence.*

**CHIMP.** Go on give us a clue

**KNUCKLE.** No chance

**CHIMP.** Go on

**KNUCKLE.** –

**CHIMP.** Go on Knucks

**KNUCKLE.** No no! No way!

**CHIMP.** You never want to tell me

**KNUCKLE.** Wonder why!

**CHIMP.** Don't trust me

**KNUCKLE.** Not as far as I can throw you

**CHIMP.** Not fair I'm a very trustworthy person

**KNUCKLE.** How'd you work that out then cos/ I tell you

**CHIMP.** I've never been late to work

**KNUCKLE.** You don't have to wake up early

**CHIMP.** I still have to wake up

**KNUCKLE.** How

**CHIMP.** I sleep during the day don't I… don't you don't you sleep during the day? When do you sleep if you don't sleep during the day?

**KNUCKE.** Never you mind when I sleep

**CHIMP.** But-

**KNUCKLE.** I sleep

**CHIMP.** –

**KNUCKLE.** Not long… no no I only sleep a few hours me all I need but I sleep the odd hour or so just enough to recharge the batteries and that

**CHIMP.** Well I make sure I get my eight hours

**KNUCKLE.** –

**CHIMP.** I've got to have my eight hours or Sal reckons I get grumpy she's right actually it's the same with tea if I've not had my cup of tea I get pretty moody… I'll bite your head off an all… I do… it's awful

**KNUCKLE.** –

**CHIMP.** Sometimes wish I drank coffee cos of it

**KNUCKLE.** No one's stopping you Chimp

**CHIMP.** Don't like it

*KNUCKLE shakes his head.*

**CHIMP.** Wish I did it's cooler isn't though – sexier – movie stars drink coffee – not tea

**KNUCKLE.** Movie stars

**CHIMP.** Sure

**KNUCKLE.** You know any movie stars Chimp

**CHIMP.** Sure. Sure I do

**KNUCKLE.** –

**CHIMP.** From the adverts/ and that

**KNUCKLE.** You talking 'bout those coffee adverts

**CHIMP.** Yeah right like/ those-

**KNUCKLE.** Do know they are being paid- for the adverts don't you Chimp?

**CHIMP.** Oh right yeah of course – I know that –

**KNUCKLE.** ?

**CHIMP.** I did know that

**KNUCKLE.** –

**CHIMP.** I did but they do look sexy

**KNUCKLE.** –

**CHIMP.** In the adverts or whatever it's very clever advertising obviously I mean take this conversation for instance that advert is somewhere in my self-conscious isn't it so obviously whoever been doing those…well they been doing their job haven't they- they have I think cos I don't really remember much but I clearly remember that…

**KNUCKLE.** –

**CHIMP.** So…

*Silence.*

*CHIMP is lying on the floor face to the ceiling.*

*He's spinning.*

**CHIMP.** Shit

**KNUCKLE.** –

**CHIMP.** This always happens when

**KNUCKLE.** –

**CHIMP.** Fuck

**KNUCKLE.** What's the matter with you?

**CHIMP.** I need a –

*KNUCKLE shakes his head.*

**CHIMP.** Number two don't I – I need a number two

**KNUCKLE.** A shit you need a shit

**CHIMP.** Right

**KNUCKLE.** Well go for one

**CHIMP.** Where

**KNUCKLE.** Go in the sink

**CHIMP.** No way

**KNUCKLE.** 'sfine! Wash it away after

**CHIMP.** –

**KNUCKLE.** Just run the hot water till it disintegrates away

**CHIMP.** You've done it before

**KNUCKLE.** Yes so what

**CHIMP.** Not doing that

**KNUCKLE.** Suit yourself

**CHIMP.** Disgusting

**KNUCKLE.** Fine… suffer

**CHIMP.** 'sjust wrong

**KNUCKLE.** Martyr

**CHIMP.** Disrespectful

**KNUCKLE.** Who too?

**CHIMP.** Owner

*Pause.*

*CHIMP is shaking again.*

*Holds his stomach and rocks.*

**KNUCKLE.** Now you see this is the same as when you go abroad on the beach

**CHIMP.** –

**KNUCKLE.** People worry about all sorts of things don't they on the beach

**CHIMP.** Do they?

**KNUCKLE.** And… why

**CHIMP.** Exposing I guess – vulnerable

**KNUCKLE.** But it shouldn't be

**CHIMP.** –

**KNUCKLE.** a) everyone else is also half fucking naked and b) you'll never see any of them again anyway

*Pause.*

**CHIMP.** So what you're saying is

**KNUCKLE.** That the owner shits too and you're never gonna meet him anyway

**CHIMP.** Might

**KNUCKLE.** Why would you be meeting the owner Chimp we never meet the owner – you're not going to be-

**CHIMP.** Alright! Alright!

*Pause.*

**KNUCKLE.** So go on then

**CHIMP.** ?

**KNUCKLE.** Take em down then

**CHIMP.** No no way

*Pause.*

**KNUCKLE.** Baby

**CHIMP.** No! I just – I don't need one now-

**KNUCKLE.** Really

**CHIMP.** Yes really thanks Knuckle-head

*CHIMP takes out a hip flask.*

*Tries to hide it from KNUCKLE but he's seen it.*

*Silence.*
*CHIMP sits gingerly down on the ground again.*

*He is sweating.*

**KNUCKLE.** Listen seriously have you been drinking

**CHIMP.** Had a vodka and cranberry before-

**KNUCKLE.** I saw you drink

**CHIMP.** What that

**KNUCKLE.** –

**CHIMP.** It's only some-

*Pause.*

**CHIMP.** 'snothing

**KNUCKLE.** –

**CHIMP.** Honestly

**KNUCKLE.** Not the way forward you've got to get your head in the game. Why are you doing this to yourself?

*Silence.*

**KNUCKLE.** Whatever this is… whatever the matter is with ya… why are you doing this to yourself… eh Chimp?

*Pause.*

**CHIMP.** I don't know – I just don't know – I'm lost in space

**KNUCKLE.** –

**CHIMP.** I don't- life is just getting tough – I don't know where to move from here

**KNUCKLE.** When did this happen

**CHIMP.** –

**KNUCKLE.** Why didn't you talk- to me

**CHIMP.** It's nothing

**KNUCKLE.** How long/ have you been

**CHIMP.** I'm just a little out of sorts is all

**KNUCKLE.** You're meant to be fit – ready

**CHIMP.** Am

**KNUCKLE.** Not if you're mind is – not how it works

**CHIMP.** S'fine

**KNUCKLE.** –

**CHIMP.** It's nothing

**KNUCKLE.** –

**CHIMP.** I'm fine

*Silence.*

**KNUCKLE.** Is it the lack of sex?

**CHIMP.** –

**KNUCKLE.** I know how that can affect a man

**CHIMP.** –

**KNUCKLE.** Affected me badly

**CHIMP.** –

**KNUCKLE.** But you've got to find other ways round it or take a step back look at yourself ask yourself why she doesn't want to have sex anymore maybe she feels under appreciated

**CHIMP.** –

**KNUCKLE.** Chimp have you considered that? Have you thought about whether Sal's felt… if she feels a sense of worth or not… does she feel wanted?

**CHIMP.** –

**KNUCKLE.** Chimp

**CHIMP.** –

**KNUCKLE.** ?

*Pause.*

**CHIMP.** It's not that

**KNUCKLE.** –

**CHIMP.** Well

**KNUCKLE.** –

**CHIMP.** But it's- it's not her- it's not her it's- it's me

**KNUCKLE.** ?

**CHIMP.** I'm the one – you know

**KNUCKLE.** I see

**CHIMP.** I just don't want to do it

**KNUCKLE.** –

**CHIMP.** I mean I see women everywhere I go… even those I don't find attractive you know before or whatever yeah like now… now I suddenly… I suddenly do now

**KNUCKLE.** –

**CHIMP.** But with Sal

**KNUCKLE.** –

**CHIMP.** I've not done anything with…not since – like you said – but not since

*KNUCKLE turns away from CHIMP.*

**CHIMP.** 'swhy I didn't say anything!

**KNUCKLE.** –

**CHIMP.** Makes me feel bad

**KNUCKLE.** That's you that not me

**CHIMP.** –

*Silence.*

*KNUCKLE hangs his head for some time until looking out.*

**KNUCKLE.** How long?

**CHIMP.** ?

*KNUCKLE looks at CHIMP.*

**KNUCKLE.** Since you and Sal

**CHIMP.** Month

**KNUCKLE.** ?

**CHIMP.** Six or so

**KNUCKLE.** Weeks

**CHIMP.** Months

**KNUCKLE.** Jeez

**CHIMP.** Alright!

*Silence.*

*KNUCKLE looks out.*

**KNUCKLE.** It's not the end of the world all that

**CHIMP.** –

**KNUCKLE.** Oh now I know some people you meet and all they care about is sex, sex, sex, but you get older and you realise it's not the be all and end all… get to a certain point… your mindset changes in a way… I'm not saying… will for you but you just… perspective… and all… it's all just about perspective. Growing up *(Pause)* understand?

**CHIMP.** Sure

**KNUCKLE.** So it may well not be the end for you… for you and Sal I mean

*Silence.*

**KNUCKLE.** Unless. Unless of course I mean… is that what you want? Maybe it is and I'm not here to judge you. No one is really Chimp we only ever judge ourselves… in a way

**CHIMP.** –

*Silence.*

**CHIMP.** I don't want that

*Silence.*

**CHIMP.** That's not what I want
*Pause.*

**KNUCKLE.** Right – well – you must tell her that then

*Silence.*

**KNUCKLE.** I've always been very careful in love

**CHIMP.** –

**KNUCKLE.** Not ever really taken–

**CHIMP.** –

**KNUCKLE.** Not my style

**CHIMP.** –

**KNUCKLE.** Often think I'm better when in a relationship. You know what I mean? But then I think back to the ones I was in and I'm sure I spent most of the time wishing more than anything not to be in them and then well then… well… then with… I… with–

*Pause.*

Life's too short for all that. Then with… my decision was made for me wasn't it and now…! I've no choice but to be alone

**CHIMP.** Not true

**KNUCKLE.** It is to me

**CHIMP.** –

**KNUCKLE.** It's a kind of respect I have now

**CHIMP.** ?

**KNUCKLE.** Anything else would be a kind of well it'd seem disrespectful I'm not in the habit of showing disrespect if I can... you know

*Silence.*

*CHIMP has a very dry throat.*

*He's more in the room now.*

**KNUCKLE.** Chimp

**CHIMP.** ?

**KNUCKLE.** I want you to know...

*Pause.*

**CHIMP.** Knucks

**KNUCKLE.** Just let me

**CHIMP.** Jesus Knucks!

**KNUCKLE.** Now come on now... don't give me all... I'm trying to tell you something

**CHIMP.** What is it spit it out

**KNUCKLE.** I think it's important for you to be aware of… of certain… things that –

**CHIMP.** ?

**KNUCKLE.** You're not a bad lad. Alright?

**CHIMP.** –

**KNUCKLE.** As far as people are concerned I've met some stinkers in my time some right stinkers I mean it all sorts I've had the pleasure and the pain to mingle with all sorts some for work some for other reasons a mixture of… realities and when it comes down to it Chimp my boy you're not a bad egg

*Pause.*

**CHIMP.** Is that –

*Pause.*

**CHIMP.** Right no. Thanks Knucks love you too mate

**KNUCKLE.** Don't you get all soft on me - you know I don't go in for all that new age man love

**CHIMP.** ?

**KNUCKLE.** What was that?

**CHIMP.** ?

*KNCKLE mouths to listen. CHIMP shuts his eyes.*

**KNUCKLE.** What you shutting your eyes for!

**CHIMP.** Helps me hear – strengthens the senses

**KNUCKLE.** Nonsense

**CHIMP.** Shh!

*They listen.*

**CHIMP.** Nothing

**KNUCKLE.** Probably a cat

**CHIMP.** It was nothing

**KNUCKLE.** Yeah probably a cat

**CHIMP.** No there was nothing

**KNUCKLE.** What do you mean?

**CHIMP.** There was nothing

**KNUCKLE.** I heard something

**CHIMP.** No you thought you heard something

**KNUCKLE.** No I heard something that was most likely a cat

**CHIMP.** Or nothing

**KNUCKLE.** It was probably a cat

**CHIMP.** There was nothing there

**KNUCKLE.** Where

**CHIMP.** When we listened

**KNUCKLE.** Yeah after I heard it

**CHIMP.** What

**KNUCKLE.** I heard and then we listened

**CHIMP.** And there was nothing

**KNUCKLE.** Yes but before

**CHIMP.** Before what

**KNUCKLE.** FOR!

**CHIMP.** ?

**KNUCKLE.** Let's leave it – it was probably nothing

**CHIMP.** Yeah exactly

**KNUCKLE.** I'm not saying it was just nothing – it was most likely a cat

**CHIMP.** You can't just say something like that based on something you think you heard

**KNUCKLE.** Know

**CHIMP.** You can't know it

**KNUCKLE.** Well I do

**CHIMP.** Not possible

**KNUCKLE.** Well it is

**CHIMP.** Not

**KNUCKLE.** –

**CHIMP.** Then you'd know if it was a cat or not wouldn't you

*Pause.*

**KNUCKLE.** It was likely to be a cat yes

**CHIMP.** You can't possibly say that

**KNUCKLE.** Watch me

*Pause.*

**CHIMP.** All I'm saying is if you can't be certain-

**KNUCKLE.** Let it go Chimp would you

**CHIMP.** But-

**KNUCKLE.** Let it go

**CHIMP.** Alright.

**KNUCKLE.** No point arguing over a little pussy cat

**CHIMP.** You-

**KNUCKLE.** Is there?

**CHIMP.** ?

**KNUCKLE.** Eh?

**CHIMP.** No I suppose not

**KNUCKLE.** Exactly. Why let a pussy come between us

**CHIMP.** I suppose you're right

*Silence.*

*CHIMP goes to the sink and drinks from it.*

*The tap runs.*

**KNUCKLE.** You know Chill?

**CHIMP.** The blackie

*KNUCKLE nods.*

**CHIMP.** Yeah?

**KNUCKLE.** You shouldn't say that

**CHIMP.** ?

**KNUCKLE.** It's not politically correct –

**CHIMP.** –

**KNUCKLE.** –

**CHIMP.** You know what else isn't political…

**KNUCKLE.** –

**CHIMP.** Shall we leave it there?

**KNUCKLE.** How much have you had?

**CHIMP.** What does that mean?

**KNUCKLE.** Why you getting so worked up

**CHIMP.** Start asking me questions about some wog like I care

**KNUCKLE.** What

**CHIMP.** –

**KNUCKLE.** What you talking about

**CHIMP.** I'm telling you I'm fed up of it

**KNUCKLE.** –

**CHIMP.** He's an arsehole

**KNUCKLE.** Right

**CHIMP.** He looks at Sal like she's meat

*Pause.*

**KNUCKLE.** This about Sal then

**CHIMP.** It's about the niggas and the way they look at her

**KNUCKLE.** How do you look at women Chimp?

**CHIMP.** –

**KNUCKLE.** Do you wear a modesty mask Chimp?

**CHIMP.** –

**KNUCKLE.** Sorry Chimp I can't hear ya

**CHIMP.** –

**KNUCKLE.** What's the matter cat got your tongue

**CHIMP.** Don't look at 'em like they're meat

**KNUCKLE.** No you just treat them like they are don't you

**CHIMP.** You what

**KNUCKLE.** You heard me

**CHIMP.** What's your problem?

**KNUCKLE.** What's yours?

**CHIMP.** –

**KNUCKLE.** Don't be so naïve

**CHIMP.** –

**KNUCKLE.** Ignorant fucker

*Silence.*

*CHIMP is hurt.*

*He licks his wounds a little and washes his face in the sink.*

*Turns the tap off.*

*It drips.*

**CHIMP.** I don't know why you're getting so…

**KNUCKLE.** You don't eh

**CHIMP.** –

**KNUCKLE.** Just 'cos you grew up round ignorant fuckers don't mean you gotta be one yourself

**CHIMP.** –

**KNUCKLE.** What do you know about him eh anyway I mean you didn't even let me tell you what I was… sad

**CHIMP.** –

**KNUCKLE.** Poor sod's gone got ball cancer. That's right chimp the nigga's got cancer of the balls

*Silence.*

*CHIMP shakes his head to dry his hair.*

**CHIMP.** I don't see how that makes –

**KNUCKLE.** Oh you don't

**CHIMP.** I –

**KNUCKLE.** Cancer of the balls

**CHIMP.** Yeah

**KNUCKLE.** Of the balls Chimp – the balls

*Silence.*

**CHIMP.** I don't see how that doesn't not make him a wanker

**KNUCKLE.** Did I say –

**CHIMP.** No but you're acting like he's a saint just cos he got cancer doesn't mean that wipes away the fact he's a bastard

**KNUCKLE.** That's not the point

**CHIMP.** What so he's gonna have one ball is he?

**KNUCKLE.** Don't ask me

**CHIMP.** Hitler had one ball

**KNUCKLE.** What's Hitler got to do with anything?

**CHIMP.** No one goes around going oh poor Hitler he only had one ball that's why he killed all those Jews we may as well let him off

**KNUCKLE.** Who's Leon killed?

**CHIMP.** What

**KNUCKLE.** Chill – who's he killed eh?

**CHIMP.** Well no one

**KNUCKLE.** Exactly you poor fucking imbecile – are you a racist are you

**CHIMP.** Not a racist

**KNUCKLE.** Fooled me

**CHIMP.** I'm –

**KNUCKLE.** What you so angry about Chimp

**CHIMP.** –

**KNUCKLE.** Look at yourself what's missing from you're life Chimp? You're a white man grew up in a middle class household… yeah you've let yourself go… you know what your parents are working class people… their mentality… work hard… they fought hard to get the upbringing you got but you go around like you've grown up on a council estate or been sent to war – you ever been to war Chimp eh? No. Course you haven't you ignorant fucker…

**CHIMP.** Fuck you Steve fuck you – sitting on your high horse acting like some sixty year old man who's seen it all act your age and stop moping over a dead woman who didn't even love you! You, you, you, you… fool! Yeah! No she proved that by how many cocks she sucked!

*Silence.*

*KNUCKLE hangs his head.*

**CHIMP.** I'm –

**KNUCKLE.** –

**CHIMP.** Knucks

*Silence.*

*KNUCKLE looks at CHIMP.*

**KNUCKLE.** Got any of that whiskey left

*Pause.*

**KNUCKLE.** Chimp

**CHIMP.** Er- yeah – you shouldn't –

*KNUCKLE takes the hip flask.*

*Goes to take a swig.*

*Restrains himself.*

*Goes to* CHIMP.

*Pours it over him.*

*CHIMP can do nothing.*

*Drops to his knees.*

*Head into the floor.*

*Silence.*

**CHIMP.** *(Moved)* Why'd you go and do that for Knucks? What'd I do to deserve that eh? What 'cos I tell you the truth mate? Wake up. You're dead inside. We're all dead inside Knucks. Dead. You think being all political gonna change shit you're deluded mate deluded. Talk bout me like I was born with a silver spoon nah far from it Knucks far from it look at me I'm middle of the road the beige of humanity FUCK YOU STEVE FUCK YOU ALRIGHT! You know I don't need it anyway the- I don't need it anyway so-

*He flies across the room like a Bull, charging straight at KNUCKLE. Takes him by the shoulders and shakes him violently.*

**CHIMP.** SNAP OUT OF IT KNUCKS! SNAP OUT OF IT!

*They fall to the floor.*

*Silence.*

**KNUCKLE.** You've nailed me there – you're right partial to a bit of wrestling I am

**CHIMP.** –

**KNUCKLE.** That said not in the mood right now funnily enough

*KNUCKLE stands – brushes himself down.*

**KNUCKLE.** No sir

*Pause.*

**KNUCKLE.** I mean… give us a clue Knucks…! No chance!

**CHIMP.** –

**KNUCKLE.** Give us a clue!

*Pause.*

**KNUCKLE.** No chance. *(Pause)* No chance. *(Pause)* No Chance

**CHIMP.** –

**KNUCKLE.** Dear me we're really scraping the barrel now aren't we Chimp scraping the bottom of the shit heap now. Why'd we do it eh? Boredom stinks don't it Chimp – love a bit of drama that's what you want a bit of drama don't you… boredom stinks

**CHIMP.** Yeah okay I am bored

**KNUCKLE.** So am I Chimp so am I

**CHIMP.** I'm bored of you I'm bored of the posh cunts the rough cunts the immigrated cunts the British cunts I'm bored of you bored of Sal I'm bored of my voice Knucks I am for Christ! I'm bored of it all –

**KNUCKLE.** And so am I Chimp so am I. But that is life my friend it's about pain… boredom… it stinks. It repeats… the boring gets more boring… we live in the boredom… we die in the boredom… if we could only love the boredom we'd be happy but we need not to be bored don't we Chimp we need the drama get high on the pain Chimp suck it in Chimp suck it in cos the boredom's gonna get us all in the end

**CHIMP.** I'm bored of being bored

**KNUCKLE.** –

**CHIMP.** I'm tired

**KNUCKLE.** –

**CHIMP.** Body aches

**KNUCKLE.** –

**CHIMP.** Voice is

**KNUCKLE.** –

**CHIMP.** Can't breathe

**KNUCKLE.** –

**CHIMP.** Make a sound

**KNUCKLE.** –

**CHIMP.** Like prison

**KNUCKLE.** –

**CHIMP.** Over. Everything's over… it all… just plays out in front of me… no control

**KNUCKLE.** –

**CHIMP.** I've nothing really. Don't own a thing

**KNUCKLE.** –

**CHIMP.** I've nothing. Nothing is truly mine. Not even my… my thoughts are being raped too! Oh they are! Savagely! I'm in a hole! I'm in a hole!

*CHIMP screams up to the skies and out in front.*

**CHIMP.** CAN YOU NOT SEE THAT!

*Silence.*

**KNUCKLE.** You think you're the only one?

**CHIMP.** Help me? Won't someone help us?

*Pause.*

**KNUCKLE.** Find the light in dark is all you can do that's all there is…the light in the dark

**CHIMP.** That can't be all there is

**KNUCKLE.** What else can there be?

**CHIMP.** There's got to be more to it all there's got to be a way out of all this this heavy dark all of this this shit

**KNUCKLE.** This is all there is

*Silence.*

*CHIMP is folded up like a leaf – head sinking in to the floor.*

**KNUCKLE.** Get up. Come on stop it now. How much did you have to drink? You stink of it. Get up.

*CHIMP breaks down.*

**CHIMP.** I'm sorry Knucks – I'm sorry mate

**KNUCKLE.** Here now come on stop it that's enough stop it

**CHIMP.** I –

**KNUCKLE.** (I know) stop it now

**CHIMP.** Only had a couple of pints

**KNUCKLE.** Of course

**CHIMP.** Took some of the – *stuff*

**KNUCKLE.** That tranquilliser rubbish

**CHIMP.** Earlier

**KNUCKLE.** Right… you feel crap do you

**CHIMP.** I feel low… really sick

**KNUCKLE.** Right up come on up you get it's your own fault now come on now up

**CHIMP.** You're right. You're a good man Knucks a good man. A friend

**KNUCKLE.** Yeah yeah. Here sit down.

**CHIMP.** –

*Silence.*

*They sit.*

*After a moment CHIMP lays out flat.*

*His head is close to KNUCKLE but they do not touch.*

*KNUCKLE looks at CHIMP as he closes his eyes.*

*KNUCKLE looks out and smiles faintly.*

*He closes his eyes too.*

**KNUCKLE.** Know what I miss... summer holidays... growing up... long stretched out things... tarmac round the cities like liquorice... treacle... ice cream vans...

*Pause.*

Know what I love the most? Butterflies. Favourite... tell my dad I want a pet Butterfly. Butterflies my favourite animal you know he, he looks at me he sort of finds it amusing I think (yeah)... lifts my face up... just an inch... just enough for me to be looking at him square in the eye you know right close to the tip of his nose I'm talking real close... he says to me in a sort growl 'butterflies are insects not animals... you'll never 'av a pet cos you're too much of an animal yourself' *(Pause)* S'fine cos entitled to his opinion (you know)... when you say I act like an old man... cos I am Harry – and I'm calling you Harry okay. How many summers eh no no if seeing the seasons change thirty odd times don't make me an old man when life in this city is this hard – atmosphere of this… (so) tense… then I don't know Harry I've a young heart still skip in my heart. But I've hurt for too long… feeling old is comfort for me – alright? *(Silence.)* I'd have these moments you know where I'd think "I've dreamt this" only I realise later that of course I haven't I've just had that moment before where I thought I'd dreamt it before where I'd thought the same thing or… always wanna believe I dream things that'll happen… future… only… one day I woke up realised there is no future Chimp. No dreams. No past. No reality. This too heavy for you Chimp. Thought you'd offended me?

*CHIMP sits up.*

**CHIMP.** No I –

**KNUCKLE.** –

**CHIMP.** Never heard you speak so…

**KNUCKLE.** I can speak Chimp I'm a great thinker… big believer in the quiet minds you know I know so many written off people out there that've great minds but they don't speak they just listen… written off for it… if they let them get a word in edgeways they'd cut through the politics of the world like… well that's what I think

**CHIMP.** Yeah… think you're right

**KNUCKLE.** –

**CHIMP.** I think people know stuff don't they

**KNUCKLE.** That's right yeah

**CHIMP.** I know stuff

**KNUCKLE.** No I know you do

**CHIMP.** Wanna know what I know Steve… I know that I was not here and then I was and I know that I was here and then I won't be. *(Pause)* I know… the rest is just noise… blah blah rah rah blah –

**KNUCKLE.** That's funny that – I like that – you've tickled me there you have Chimp

**CHIMP.** Feel a bit brighter

**KNUCKLE.** I can tell

**CHIMP.** No I do… there's a new wave coming on… just then… felt like the sun had…

**KNUCKLE.** –

**CHIMP.** My dad was a cunt too you know

**KNUCKLE.** –

**CHIMP.** So I get it

**KNUCKLE.** –

**CHIMP.** Always tried to be like him… used to dress like him – try and be him and that's stupid really now I… but I was a kid – he was like a bear to me

**KNUCKLE.** Yeah like a –

**CHIMP.** Remember standing next to him in the toilets... some shopping centre. I'm looking over the urinals at his cock thinking how big is your cock – my dad the man with the big thing... 'that's my dad with the big cock.'

**KNUCKLE.** Then you grew up and realised did ya

**CHIMP.** That it just looked big in comparison right

**KNUCKLE.** Oh dear... the shattering revelations we have... eh?

**CHIMP.** They threw this party for my eighteenth my parents they lay everything on my dad does a bbq... weather stays nice... I stand up in front of everyone and I tell them all that I'm not going be here long. I'm going to make something of myself that I'm not going waste my time and be like my dad... didn't say that... not exactly. But I don't say thank you or... no thank you or nothing. It's just me all proud. *(Pause)* Mum told me it broke his heart said it sent him over the edge she said it's what made him go back on the...

**KNUCKLE.** None of us stop being on it you know it's called restraint

**CHIMP.** Right

**KNUCKLE.** There's no cure

**CHIMP.** No

**KNUCKLE.** Nothing can knock you back if you've got restraint and a clear head...you've got to do it for yourself if that's what you want

**CHIMP.** Sure right

*There is sudden power cut.*

**CHIMP.** There goes the power!

**KNUCKLE.** –

**CHIMP.** Like this bit –'sfun. My favourite bit the dark bit

**KNUCKLE.** Love the theatrics don't you

**CHIMP.** Yeah I do

**KNUCKLE.** Knew it

**CHIMP.** You are right I do – love it – eh listen you hear the rain?

**KNUCKLE.** It's been pouring it down since right before we got here

**CHIMP.** No I know like I know it has but listen… rain always… in the dark… sounds

**KNUCKLE.** Yeah

*They listen.*

**CHIMP.** I like the rain at this time of year it's that time of year the frogs get lost

**KNUCKLE.** Eh?

**CHIMP.** You know everywhere so wet they start hopping in places they were never made to go to and they get lost don't they or eaten by foxes

**KNUCKLE.** Never knew you were a frog expert Chimp

**CHIMP.** Yeah yeah whatever I like the rain is all

**KNUCKLE.** No. I know. I know what you mean. Yeah no the rain reminds me of something that I've no idea what

**CHIMP.** What kind of thing?

**KNUCKLE.** No I… never mind.

*They listen.*

**CHIMP.** Do you think you'll do this forever?

**KNUCKLE.** No.

**CHIMP.** Really no?

**KNUCKLE.** No I don't think I will no.

**CHIMP.** –

**KNUCKLE.** More to life

**CHIMP.** –

**KNUCKLE.** Than all this

**CHIMP.** Don't make enough do we?

**KNUCKLE.** Money

**CHIMP.** Yeah I mean we make hardly nothing

**KNUCKLE.** Not about the money that's not important

*They listen.*

**CHIMP.** Shame about Chill

**KNUCKLE.** Bout Chill's balls?

**CHIMP.** Right. Shame about Chill's balls

**KNUCKLE.** It is a shame Harry it is

**CHIMP.** Wouldn't wish one ball on no man

**KNUCKLE.** Neither would I. No

*Pause.*

*A car radio has been switched on in the distance, outside the building site... a brief moment of a male presenter speaking and then Villagers – Nothing Arrives plays.*

**KNUCKLE.** Listen they're here

**CHIMP.** Yes. They're here

*The lights flicker back on – the tap still drips.*

*The lights reveal the two men sat on the floor still.*

*They listen to the drip.*

*The music goes from muffled sounding to filling the entire space.*

*The men look out and sing along directly to the audience.*

*The song ends as the car door slams shut.*

*The car drives off.*

*Just the drip now. They listen.*

**CHIMP.** Here Knucks. Give us a clue.

**KNUCKLE.** No chance.

*The lights go out again. A knock.*

*End*